The Delaplaine
2020 Long Weekend Guide

Andrew Delaplaine

NO BUSINESS HAS PAID A SINGLE PENNY OR GIVEN _ANYTHING_ TO BE INCLUDED IN THIS BOOK.

A list of the author's other travel guides, as well as his political thrillers and titles for children, can be found at the end of this book.

Senior Editors - *Renee & Sophie Delaplaine*
Senior Writer - **James Cubby**

Gramercy Park Press
New York – London - Paris

Please submit corrections, additions or comments to
andrewdelaplaine@mac.com

NASHVILLE
The Delaplaine
Long Weekend Guide

TABLE OF CONTENTS

Chapter 1
WHY NASHVILLE?

Every city has its own nickname. (Some even have more than one.) New York is the Big Apple. New Orleans is the Big Easy. Chicago is the City of the Big Shoulders.

Nashville is Music City, pure and simple. When you hear the term Music City, you only think of one town, and that town is Nashville.

While Memphis is a larger city than Nashville, Nashville is the capital of Tennessee. I never actually thought about that till I first arrived here. My initial reaction on hearing that Nashville was the capital of Tennessee was to think how odd that sounded. I'd only thought of Nashville as the "Country Music Capital of the World," which of course it is. Not as the capital of anything else.

Having been raised in South Carolina, I well remember seeing Minnie Pearl on TV in broadcasts from the **Grand Ole Opry**, which has done weekly shows since 1925, making it the longest continuously broadcast radio show in history.

Nashville is not only the center of the country music business, but for Christian music as well.

They city has outgrown its label as a purely "country" town. What makes it particularly unique is that it combines the best elements of a small town (people say "Hello" on the streets, the clerks in the shops are as pleasant as can be) with the sophistication of a big town (the museums are superlative, the galleries cutting edge, the restaurants are world class—repeat the words **Catbird Seat** and **Rolf & Daughters** to me).

The restaurant scene has exploded, and now features some of the most original cooking that stands up to the best that New York has to offer. Just look at what they're doing at the **Catbird Seat.** I find it particularly interesting that Sean Brock, who so successfully opened Husk and McCrady's in Charleston, opted to return to Nashville (where he once worked for 3 years at the Hermitage) with a local version of **Husk**. If Brock's presence doesn't say something about the food scene in Nashville, nothing does.

The bar scene also has greatly expanded, offering much more variety. As for nightlife, there's never been anyplace with so much music going on. Start at the **Bluebird Café** (the location of scenes in ABC's "Nashville" TV show, though they use a set that recreates the site) and then dig deeper.

The formerly down-and-dirty **12 South District** has bounced back big-time with eateries offering sustainable cuisine, trendy shops, a cutting edge atmosphere, making it one of the hotter new areas of town. Meanwhile, in what's now called **SoBro** (meaning that it's directly south of the famous Broadway honky-tonk area), once home to almost nothing, you can experience a whole new neighborhood coming alive as it changes day by day, with famous chefs opening restaurants and craft cocktails being served at new hotspots.

One thing I guarantee: You'll never get Nashville out of your blood.

Chapter 2
WHERE TO STAY

404 HOTEL
404 12th Ave S, Nashville, 615-242-7404
www.the404nashville.com
Located in the Gulch neighborhood, this unique urban
oasis offers five king rooms with a mix of vintage and
custom furniture. Amenities include: gourmet pastries
delivered from nearby bakery, and in-room
refrigerators stocked with complimentary drinks.

THE DRAKE INN
420 Murfreesboro Pike, Nashville, 615-256-7770
www.drakeinnnashville.com
This two-level historic inn features 101 well-
appointed guest rooms with modern conveniences.
Amenities include: swimming pool, Jacuzzi, cable
TVs and free internet access. Conveniently located
near Downtown area, Music Row, Country Hall of
Fame and other local attractions. While there's no
restaurant on site, there are plenty of good ones
nearby. Pet-friendly hotel.

GAYLORD OPRYLAND RESORT AND CONVENTION CENTER

2800 Opryland Dr, Nashville, 615-889-1000
www.gaylordhotels.com

This resort and convention center offers 2,881 guest rooms all decorated with a Southern flair. Amenities include: free high-speed Internet access, cable TVs, movie channels, and coffeemakers. This hotel features 9 acres of indoor gardens, cascading waterfalls, an indoor river, and **indoor and outdoor swimming pools, and** a 20,000 square foot spa and fitness center. The resort features an amazing selection of on-site restaurants for the guests dining pleasure. Smoke-free hotel. It's all a little much, but if you're looking for a "one-stop shop" kind of place to stay, this would be the place.

GERMANTOWN INN

1218 6th Ave N, Nashville, 615-581-1218

www.germantowninn.com

NEIGHBORHOOD: Germantown

Luxury boutique hotel set in a converted 19th-century home offering 6 suites all named after American presidents. (The Monroe Room on the second floor is more spacious than the others, so try to get that one first.) Amenities: Complimentary Wi-Fi, flat-screen TVs, and complimentary breakfast. Features: lush outdoor courtyard and private rooftop terrace with downtown views. (This is where I went to enjoy my morning coffee when I stayed here—what a view!) Some of the hottest restaurants in town are all within walking distance, as well as interesting shopping, and the Music City Center. Broadway's honky-tonk joints are similarly within walking distance.

THE HERMITAGE HOTEL

231 Sixth Ave N, Nashville, 615-244-3121

www.thehermitagehotel.com

NEIGHBORHOOD: Downtown

Oh, what a lovely hotel. It looks like it belongs in New York City when you first pull up to it, with its majestic Beaux-Arts stone façade, the high arched windows rising from the second floor, each arch framed by double Corinthian columns. But as soon as you get out of your cab, you'll realize you're not in New York because of the Southern hospitality. It

starts right with the doorman. (Lots of musicians and people in the music industry stay here.) It's been one of the more elegant places to stay in Nashville since it opened in 1910. You'll love the ornate lobby ceiling with its soaring coffered arches, the plush chairs gathered around the fireplace. When the place opened, it had 250 rooms. But the remodeling over the years has brought the count down to 122, with renovations updating the lodgings and enlarging the rooms to between 500 and 650 square feet (larger than my first apartment in New York). From lots of the rooms you can get superlative views of Downtown as well as the State Capitol. Big marble bathrooms with double vanities; soaking tubs; separate shower; down-filled duvets; flat screen TVs, free Internet and lots of other amenities. 24-hour room service. Spa Services: massages, wraps, scrub treatments and much more. Pet friendly. Business center including secretarial services. The on-site restaurant is the **Capitol Grille**, which is very, very good, serving vegetables grown and beef raised from farms nearby. The only hotel in Tennessee that carries both the Forbes Five Star and AAA Five diamond ratings. Also has the **Oak Bar**, a great place for a meeting or even a romantic drink before or after dinner. (Tip: Has a good happy hour that attracts a lot of locals, 4:30 to 6:30.)

HILTON NASHVILLE DOWNTOWN
121 4th Ave S, Nashville, 615-620-1000
http://www3.hilton.com/en/hotels/tennessee/hilton-nashville-downtown-BNANSHF/index.html
NEIGHBORHOOD: Downtown
This all-suite hotel has an AAA Four-Diamond rating. Has undergone serious renovations to its lobby and some 300 suites. Has the faceless look of a typical businessman's hotel on the

outside, but it's nice enough inside, with a little "creek" running through the atrium-style lobby. The rooms are spic-and-span, modern, and the hotel has all the amenities (fitness room, business center) you expect at a Hilton property. Also has **Parkview Café** in the lobby, which makes a good spot for a quick (if uninspired) lunch, as well as the **Sportsgrille**, a good place to drink some beer and catch the game on one of their TVs. **The Palm Steakhouse** is worth coming to even if you're not staying here. Nothing run-of-the-mill about this place.)

HOMEWOOD SUITES
706 Church St, Nashville, 615-742-5550
https://homewoodsuites3.hilton.com
NEIGHBORHOOD: Downtown

If you're looking for an "extended stay" lodging in Downtown, Homewood Suites, located in the historic Doctor's Building, is a good bet. (If you want a little more upscale property with suites only, go to the **Hilton**—see above.) But it's also good for a Long Weekend. They only offer suites, and they come with full kitchens, free Internet and free hot breakfast.

HOTEL INDIGO
301 Union St, Nashville, 615-891-6000
http://www.ihg.com/hotelindigo/hotels/us/en/nashvill e/bnaus/hoteldetail/directions
NEIGHBORHOOD: Downtown
Located in a majestic building that used to house the Nashville Trust back in the 1920s. Not quite in the heart of Downtown, but just a few blocks away. The lobby has a "printer's theme," because the hotel is close to Printer's Row. This is not a luxury hotel, but it's still good, with a location in an historic building, a contemporary renovation that really works, an excellent on-site restaurant, the **District Bar & Kitchen**, live music downstairs off the lobby. The prices here can be very attractive, so check them out.

HUTTON HOTEL
1808 W End St, Nashville, 615-340-9333
www.huttonhotel.com
NEIGHBORHOOD: West End
It's not that impressive from the outside, but once you're inside, it's a completely different story. I love the 1950s styled stairs in the lobby. You almost expect Doris Day and Rock Hudson to walk down them, squabbling. High-end 4-Star hotel that's proud of its "green" reputation. They use highly renewable bamboo flooring and furnishings; card readers that turn out the lights when you leave the room—the rooms, by the way, are notably spacious; LED lighting throughout the hotel; dual flush toilets, etc. In their excellent on-site **1808 Grille**, reclaimed wood is used in the décor (to very great advantage, I might add). The 250 room and 50 suites are super contemporary in design, with lots of high-tech amenities; coffee maker in the room; hair dryers; media hubs; plush robes and the like. 24-hour room service from the 1808 Grille.

LOEWS VANDERBILT HOTEL
2100 W End Ave, Nashville, 615-320-1700
www.loewshotels.com/vanderbilt
NEIGHBORHOOD: West End
Right across from Vanderbilt U, this is a AAA Four
Diamond property, and has been for decades. It's big,
with 340 rooms, 14 very fine suites. The list of
amenities goes on and on. Stay on the Club Level and
get access to their 2-story Concierge Lounge on the
top two floors, with extras like expanded Continental
breakfast (with egg), fresh fruits, pastries, etc. you
can get coffee, tea and snacks all day, and free beer
and wine and canapés at cocktail hour. There's also
an excellent view of the university from these high
floors. The hotel has a fine restaurant on site as well,
Mason's, which serves a kind of "Southern
Brasserie" cuisine, which take traditionally French
dishes and gives them a Southern twist. The bar here
has a lively scene as well.

MILLENNIUM MAXWELL HOUSE HOTEL
PRINCE'S HOT CHICKEN SHACK
5814 Nolensville Pike, Nashville, 615-810-9388
https://princeshotchicken.com
CUISINE: Southern
DRINKS: No Booze
SERVING: Lunch, Dinner; closed Sunday
PRICE RANGE: $

Known as the pioneer of Hot Chicken, this place serves a variety of Hot Chicken in pieces, strips or whole. It's quite popular so expect a wait. The story goes that back in the 1930s, Thornton Prince came home very late after cheating on his girlfriend. To get back at him, she gave him fried chicken loaded down with cayenne pepper. Her trick backfired, because he loved it. He even opened the country's first "hot chicken" place in the mid-1930s. If you can handle the heat, you'll find the chicken they fry is moist and juicy inside. They will warn you not to touch your eyes after eating this chicken.

Rosa L Parks Blvd, Nashville, 615-259-4343
www.millenniumhotels.com
This property has a "Country Music" theme, so if
you're into country music (and why else would you
come to Nashville if you weren't?), this makes an
excellent choice.

MUSIC CITY HOSTEL
1809 Patterson St, Nashville, 615-497-1208
www.musiccityhostel.com
This budget alternative offers shared dorm rooms as
well as private rooms.

NASHVILLE FARM STAY
8528 Lewis Rd, Bellevue, 615-810-8712
www.nashvillefarmstay.com
Located on 6 acres and surrounded by beautiful oak
and maple trees, this newly renovated 3-bedroom
home offers a great alternative to hotels out in rural
Bellevue. The home is completely furnished and
features a front screened-in porch and a backyard
with a full patio. Located one mile from the **Natchez
Trace Parkway**, this urban retreat is also close to
eateries like the legendary **Loveless Café**.

SCARRITT-BENNET CENTER
1027 18th Ave S, Nashville, 615-340-7500
www.scarrittbennett.org
This is another budget property that offers private
rooms, but you have to share a bathroom. Close to
Vanderbilt and Music Row.

THE UNION STATION HOTEL
1001 Broadway, 615-726-1001
www.unionstationhotelnashville.com
Formerly a railroad station, this hidden gem is
breathtaking from the moment you enter the lobby
with its 65-foot barrel-vaulted ceiling. The recently
renovated hotel offers 125 guest rooms and 12 deluxe
suites. Amenities include: LCD flat screen TVs, high-
speed wireless Internet access, Pay-Per-View and
Web TV, coffeemaker with coffee, and free daily
newspaper. On-site cocktails and dining is available
at the **Prime 108 Lounge** and **Prime 108
Restaurant**. Conveniently located near attractions
like Ryman Auditorium and LP Field. Smoke-free
hotel.

Chapter 3
WHERE TO EAT

3 CROW BAR
1024 Woodland St, Nashville, 615-262-3345
www.3crowbar.com
CUISINE: Sandwiches/Bar Grub
DRINKS: Full bar
SERVING: Lunch/Dinner/Late Night
PRICE RANGE: $
NEIGHBORHOOD: East End
Popular locals' hangout with happy hour specials and trivia nights. Bar menu includes delicious sandwiches like the Steak Sandwich served with loaded baked potato salad. Excellent draft beer selection.

12 SOUTH TAPROOM AND GRILL
2318 12th Ave S, Nashville, 615-463-7552
www.12southtaproom.com
CUISINE: American (New)
DRINKS: Beer & Wine
SERVING: Lunch, Dinner, Closed Sunday

PRICE RANGE: $$
NEIGHBORHOOD: Belmont/Hillsboro

This is a popular spot for locals serving great food
and cocktails. Their beer list is extensive, and I'd
guess they have the biggest selection representing
Nashville's small-batch breweries. The grill's menu
includes everything from burgers to tacos,
sandwiches and burritos. Menu favorites include:
Grilled Salmon and the Garlic Stuffed Roasted Pork
Loin. Vegetarian options available.

404 KITCHEN
507 12th Ave S, Nashville, 615-251-1404
www.the404nashville.com
CUISINE: American
DRINKS: Full Bar
SERVING: Dinner, Closed Sun & Mon

PRICE RANGE: $$$
NEIGHBORHOOD: Downtown; Gulch
Located next to the **Station Inn** in a former shipping
container (that's right, a real shipping container), this
very small eatery (about 40 seats) offers a menu of
modern classic European cuisine. Menu favorites
include: Glendale Farms Chicken leg confit and
Peach and Pork Ragout. The impressive Chef Matt
Bolus runs the place, which features indoor and
outdoor dining.

ARNOLD'S COUNTRY KITCHEN
605 8th Ave S, Nashville, 615-256-4455
www.arnoldscountrykitchen.com
CUISINE: Southern
DRINKS: No Booze
SERVING: **Lunch only**, Closed Sat & Sun
PRICE RANGE: $
NEIGHBORHOOD: Downtown

This place is always busy so expect a line. The menu changes daily with favorites like Chicken and Dumplings, Meatloaf, and BBQ Chicken and Catfish. Here you'll find authentic Southern dishes served in a "meat plus three" style (that's meat plus three sides for all you non-Southerners). You will dine family-style.

BISCUIT LOVE
316 11th Ave S., Nashville, 615-490-9584
www.biscuitlove.com
CUISINE: Southern/American Traditional
DRINKS: Beer & Wine Only
SERVING: Breakfast & Lunch
PRICE RANGE: $$
NEIGHBORHOOD: The Gulch/Downtown
This locals' favorite is an offshoot of a food truck that offers a menu of Southern fare – breakfast and lunch. There's always a line but the wait is well worth it. Menu treats include: Southern Benny (a Southern take on Eggs Benedict) and Donuts (specialty donuts made with lemon icing). Mimosas are made from freshly squeezed orange juice.

BLACK RABBIT
218 3rd Ave N, Nashville, 615-891-2380
www.blackrabbittn.com
CUISINE: Tapas/Small Plates
DRINKS: Full Bar
SERVING: Breakfast, Lunch, Dinner
PRICE RANGE: $$
NEIGHBORHOOD: Downtown

Chic eatery in an 1890s building with brick walls and wooden floors near Printers Alley (where Nashville's publishing industry got started 120 years ago) offering a menu of New American small plates and tacos. The owners wanted to simulate an early 20th Century vibe, with handcrafted cocktails and music (live acts every night, usually jazz, sometimes played on a century-old piano), but it's really quite modern. The wood-roasted rabbit sliders are just perfectly delicious. All breads are homemade, the meats are cured in the basement below and a lot of ingredients get the scent of hickory on the grill. As impressive as the cuisine is, the cocktails are the star attraction here. Try the "Lost in Hell's Kitchen" - an aged rum Manhattan. Large list of impressive cocktails.

BROWN'S DINER
2102 Blair Blvd, Nashville, 615-269-5509
www.brownsdiner.com
WEBSITE DOWN AT PRESSTIME
CUISINE: Diner/Dive Bar
DRINKS: Beer & Wine Only
SERVING: Lunch/Dinner
PRICE RANGE: $
NEIGHBORHOOD: Hillsboro West End
A no-frills family run diner that offers "honest to goodness" diner fare. Of course the menu features hamburgers, hot dogs, hush puppies, and frito chili pies. Winner of "Best Cheeseburger" awards for many years and rightly so.

BUTCHER & BEE
902 Main St, 615-226-3322

www.butcherandbee.com
CUISINE: American (New) / Southern / Middle Eastern
DRINKS: Full Bar
SERVING: Lunch & Dinner
PRICE RANGE: $$
NEIGHBORHOOD: East Nashville/ Edgefield
Casual eatery offering everything from sandwiches to Middle Eastern fare. It started off with the interesting idea of making sandwiches with the same approach top-flight chefs handle the farm-to-table concept: use only the finest ingredients, but do it not with white tablecloths, or fancy European-style cuisine—do it with sandwiches. "A gourmet meal between two pieces of bread" about sums up their attitude. Well, it worked, and now they offer a varied menu with some interesting Middle Eastern twists far beyond the sandwiches (which are still a huge draw here, no question). They have 2 bars here, one with stools facing a regular liquor bar and the other facing the kitchen. Raw bare-beamed ceilings crisscrossed with exposed a/c ductwork gives the place an industrial feel. Favorites: Snapper Ceviche and Avocado Crispy Rice. The Bacon-wrapped dates and Lamb meatballs are worth trying. Impressive beer and wine list. Creative cocktails.

BUTCHERTOWN HALL
1416 4th Ave N, Nashville, 615-454-3634
www.butchertownhall.com
CUISINE: Pizza, Mediterranean
DRINKS: Beer & Wine Only
SERVING: Dinner; closed Mondays

PRICE RANGE: $$
NEIGHBORHOOD: Germantown
Rustic-chic New American eatery featuring a beer
garden for wood-fired & smoked meats. Favorites:
Brisket tacos and Smoked turkey breast sandwich.
Page-long selection of beers.

CAFÉ ROZE
1115 Porter Rd, 615-645-9100
www.caferoze.com
CUISINE: American (New)
DRINKS: Full Bar
SERVING: Breakfast, Lunch, & Dinner
PRICE RANGE: $$
NEIGHBORHOOD: East Side
Trendy café with floor-to-ceiling windows looking
out into the street. White marble-topped bar gives the
place a clean, sleek look. On the other wall of the
narrow room is a long banquette below a bare white
wall broken up by some unusual modern light
fixtures. Not a single piece of art on any surface. This
rather severe sounding look is actually very sleek,
very cool. Offers an all-day menu of creative
American classics. Popular brunch spot. Favorites:
Corn fritters; Chili eggplant; Steak frites; Harissa
Chicken (with creamy polenta); Pinewood Farms
Grass Fed Burger.

CAFFÉ NONNA
4427 Murphy Rd, 615-463-0133
www.caffenonna.com
CUISINE: Italian
DRINKS: Wine & Beer

SERVING: Dinner, Closed Sundays
PRICE RANGE: $$
NEIGHBORHOOD: Sylvan Park
Long-time no-frills locals' favorite for classic Italian fare. Where you go when you want basic Italian comfort food in a simple atmosphere. Dark enough at night so it can actually feel intimate, though there's nothing distinctive about the décor. Favorites: Fettuccine Alfredo and Lasagna Bolognese. The Tiramisu is a must-try, but my favorite was the Pumpkin ricotta cheesecake. Small basic wine list.

CAPITOL GRILLE
THE HERMITAGE HOTEL
231 Sixth Ave N, Nashville, 615-345-7116
www.thehermitagehotel.com
CUISINE: American
DRINKS: Full Bar

SERVING: Breakfast (from 6:30), Lunch & Dinner daily
PRICE RANGE: $$$$
NEIGHBORHOOD: Downtown

As I said above in the listing for the hotel where this dark-ceilinged dining room is housed, the Chef, Tyler Brown, who also owns the farm, grows the vegetables served here. The beef? Raised by Double H Farms just outside town, owned by the Heritage Hotel. Tyler changes his menus with the seasons to reflect what he can get fresh. Between the high arches are murals depicting Nashville scenes. House-cured country ham chowder; venison loin served with apples and parsnips; short rib pot roast; Brussels sprouts with bacon and brown sugar (I've never had Brussels sprouts served like this—just delicious); for dessert try the peanut butter chocolate chess pie served with banana ice cream and peanut brittle. Oh, and the charming **Oak Bar** located here, always an excellent choice for a drink.

CATBIRD SEAT
1711 Division St, Nashville, 615-810-8200

www.thecatbirdseatrestaurant.com
CUISINE: American
DRINKS: Full bar; $30 corkage fee (ouch!) if you
bring your own wine
SERVING: Dinner Wednesday-Sunday; closed
Monday & Tuesday; reservations from 5:30; last
reservations at 9:15
PRICE RANGE: $$$$

They have a couple of booths against the wall, but
most people want one of the 20 seats at the square-
shaped counter surrounding the open kitchen, where
the chef & his team make your multi-course meal
(over $100 per person, but it includes wine and
booze, so it's not as expensive as it sounds) while you
watch. Whichever chef makes the course will deliver
it to you personally so you can ask questions. There's
no menu and you won't be able to find out what
you're eating till you get there. But this is one of the
hottest tickets in Nashville. It's next to the **Patterson
House.** The food is exquisite, and if you can bear up
to 3 hours to get through the experience, you will be
handsomely rewarded. Expect items like: aged
roasted duck; pork sandwich; duck breast with
strawberries & almonds; hot & spicy chicken skins;
crisp country ham; oyster with seaweed; snapper
poached with chorizo; sea urchin with beets; charcoal
grilled turbot. The desserts are standouts.

You have to reserve on their web site. Reservation
dates open up 30 days in advance. If you cancel, you
have to do so 7 days before your reservation or pay a
$75 fee. Walk-ins are not accepted.

CHAUHAN ALE & MASALA HOUSE

123 12th Ave N, 615-242-8426

www.chauhannashville.com

CUISINE: Indian/Southern

DRINKS: Full Bar

SERVING: Lunch & Dinner, Brunch and Dinner on weekends

PRICE RANGE: $$

NEIGHBORHOOD: The Gulch

Located in a refurbished garage, this dark room with walls covered with red brick here and colorful tiles over there has a lot of charm. High ceilings, exposed beams on one side of a partition that divides the room, with a white-painted ceiling on the other side, a fireplace, quirky lighting fixtures overhead—all of this adds to the fun, funky atmosphere. This eatery serves creative Indian fare and comfort classics. Favorites: Tandoori Chicken Poutine; Tandoori baked brie; Hot chicken pakoras; Tamarind lamb chop; and the award-winning Chauhan Burger. Impressive list of wines and spirits. I'll wager you've never had any of the desserts, so you'll want to order them all.

CITY HOUSE

1222 4th Ave N, Nashville, 615-736-5838

www.cityhousenashville.com

CUISINE: Italian
DRINKS; Full Bar
SERVING: Dinner
PRICE RANGE: $$$
NEIGHBORHOOD: Germantown
Chef Tandy Wilson has an Italian menu with a lot of
Southern twists. He believes in the "snout to tail"
approach when it comes to animals, and that's why he
gets in whole pigs and uses every bit of them. You'll
find his house-cured sausage in a pasta dish and then
find ham from the pig's belly on one of his pizzas
(the pizzas are unlike any you've ever had). Based on
what I've said so far, you'll want to focus on the
charcuterie items here in his big open room with brick
walls that formerly was a sculptor's studio.

CRYING WOLF
823 Woodland St, Nashville, 615-953-6715
www.thecryingwolf.com
CUISINE: Burgers
DRINKS: Full Bar
SERVING: Dinner
PRICE RANGE: $$
NEIGHBORHOOD: Edgefield
A no-frills bar that serves burgers. There's a deck, a
dart board and a juke box.

CZANN'S BREWING CO.
505 Lea Ave, Nashville, 615-748-1399
www.czanns.com
CUISINE: Pizza/Brewery
DRINKS: Beer Only

SERVING: Lunch & Dinner Sat & Sun; Dinner only
Thu & Fri; Closed Mon - Wed
PRICE RANGE: $
NEIGHBORHOOD: Sobro, Downtown
This newly opened brewery offers a room for tasting
its wares. No frills, no tours, and only 5 beers on tap.
No dinner menu but they do serve pizza.

DINO'S
411 Gallatin Ave, Nashville, 615-226-3566
www.dinosnashville.com
CUISINE: Breakfast/Burgers
DRINKS: Full bar
SERVING: Dinner & Late Night
PRICE RANGE: $
NEIGHBORHOOD: Lockeland Springs
An old-school dive bar that serves cheap beer and
burgers. Tip: Order your food at the register when
you walk in and then find a seat. Beer and fries –
that's the menu.

DOZEN BAKERY
516 Hagan St #103, 615-712-8150
www.dozen-nashville.com
CUISINE: Bakery/Sandwiches
DRINKS: No Booze
SERVING: 7 a.m. – 6 p.m.
PRICE RANGE: $$
NEIGHBORHOOD: Wedgewood-Houston
Simple counter-serve (pick up your order and go to a
table) bakery featuring fresh baked breads (baguettes,
sourdough, rye, challah and more) and sweets along
with breakfast and sandwiches. Arrive early if you're

pastry shopping. For b'fast, get a split baguette with Benton's bacon, scrambled eggs or just with homemade jam. Lunch could be a hot Cuban sandwich or salami or eggplant. It's all wonderfully good. Try the fluffy Almond croissant and the oatmeal/cranberry cookie. Brunch served on weekends.

EDLEY'S BAR-B-QUE
2706 12th Ave S, Nashville, 615-953-2951
www.edleysbbq.com
CUISINE: Barbeque
DRINKS: Full Bar
SERVING: Lunch, Dinner
PRICE RANGE: $$
NEIGHBORHOOD: Belmont/Hillsboro
Lovers of BBQ flock to this Nashville institution for the food and hospitality. Menu favorites include: Pork Tacos and the Catfish sandwich. The meats are smoked fresh daily and they also serve homemade baked beans, mac and cheese, and cornbread.

EPICE
2902 12th Ave S, Nashville, 615-720-6765
www.epicenashville.com
CUISINE: Lebanese
DRINKS: Full Bar
SERVING: Lunch, Dinner
PRICE RANGE: $$
NEIGHBORHOOD: 12 South
Lovely eatery featuring nice selection of Lebanese fare. Menu favorites include: Tabouli, hummus, and

the Eggplant and lamb with vermicelli rice. Imported wines.

ETCH
303 Demonbreun St, Nashville, 615-522-0685
www.etchrestaurant.com
CUISINE: New American
DRINKS: Full Bar
SERVING: Lunch weekdays (11-2 only); dinner nightly except Sunday, when it's closed
PRICE RANGE: $$$ to $$$$
NEIGHBORHOOD: Downtown
A classy, upscale restaurant serving food from what I consider to be one of the top 2 or 3 menus in Nashville. There's an open kitchen with seats at the bar so you can interact with the staff (if you care to). If you'd rather share an intimate meal with someone, go to one of the tables. Scallops on a bed of greens; octopus & shrimp bruschetta; rutabaga la plancha

(simply wonderful); a grilled lamb T-bone; tempura okra; a sensational creation called the "Charcuterie Salad" consisting of Tennessee prosciutto, house cured sausages, yellow beet mustard puree, greens, spiced vinaigrette, smoked lima beans, pickled onion, apple confit, fried oyster mushrooms—you've never had a salad like this before. The desserts are similarly creative: white chocolate lemon ganache.

FIDO
1812 21st Ave S, Nashville, 615-777-3436
www.bongojava.com/fido-cafe
CUISINE: American; comfort
DRINKS: Beer & Wine
SERVING: Breakfast, Lunch, Dinner
PRICE RANGE: $$
NEIGHBORHOOD: Hillsboro/West End
This casual café offers a varied menu of organic, exotic and junk foods. Menu favorites include: the famous Local Burger (a mixture of beef & lamb) and the Liberal Salad. All desserts are made in-house. Breakfast is served all day.

FOLK
823 Meridian St, 615-610-2595
www.goodasfolk.com
CUISINE: American (New)
DRINKS: Full Bar
SERVING: Dinner
PRICE RANGE: $$
NEIGHBORHOOD: McFerrin Park
You walk by a stack of split wood on you way to the front door, and the scent tells you this wood is going

to end up in the wood-burning oven where they make
the great pizzas here. Casual eatery offering a creative
menu of American fare and pizza. But they have a lot
more to offer than pizza: Chicken Milanese; Heritage
pork with cranberry beans; Half chicken Milanese
(this is very tasty); and Beef tartare. Get a side order
of the marinated Cerignola olives. (One of my
favorite types of olive.) Impressive bourbon list.

FROTHY MONKEY
2509 12th Ave S, Nashville, 615-600-4756
www.frothymonkey.com
Has other locations in Nashville
CUISINE: American; coffeeshop; sandwich shop
DRINKS: Beer & Wine only
SERVING: Breakfast (from 7 am), Lunch & Dinner
(till 9 pm)
PRICE RANGE: $

NEIGHBORHOOD: Belmont / Hillsboro / 12 South
Very reasonably priced place for a meal any time. Not
only is it cheap, but they're very serious about the

sustainability of what their serve here. They have gluten-free options, vegetarian & vegan dishes, a special kids' menu, craft-inspired beer & wine list. They support local vendors & suppliers. Look for the sign out front with the monkey holding a coffee mug. Biscuits and gravy with eggs; smoky asparagus & kale soup; French toast & waffles; great selection of salads and hot and cold sandwiches. For dinner, they have cider glazed pork with cinnamon sweet potatoes; blackened shrimp & grits; a sausage burger and blackened Gulf mahi. Also some great gift items from their store: crocheted monkeys and other items.

GIOVANNI'S RISTORANTE
909 20th Ave S, Nashville, 615-760-5932
www.giovanninashville.com
CUISINE: Italian
DRINKS: Full Bar
SERVING: Lunch & Dinner
PRICE RANGE: $$$$
NEIGHBORHOOD: Midtown
You can get really sublime Italian cuisine here. Giovanni is one of the stars of the burgeoning restaurant scene here in Nashville. An elegant room with white tablecloths and fine crystal with lovely arched windows looking outside. They have a traditional menu that touches all the bases, but what's special here is how expertly everything is prepared.

GREKO GREEK STREET FOOD
704 Main St, 615-203-0251
www.grekostreetfood.com
CUISINE: Greek/Mediterranean

DRINKS: Beer & Wine
SERVING: Lunch & Dinner
PRICE RANGE: $$
NEIGHBORHOOD: East Nashville
Casual no-frills eatery offering authentic
Greek/Mediterranean fare. Favorites: Athenian
chicken with peasant rice and Monastiraki-Style Beef.
Variety of Souvlaki skewers. Open kitchen and
communal tables. Greek wines.

HATTIE B'S
112 19th Ave S, Nashville, 615-678-4794
www.hattieb.com
CUISINE: American, Southern, Soul Food
DRINKS: Beer & Wine
SERVING: Lunch, Dinner

PRICE RANGE: $
NEIGHBORHOOD: Belmont/Vanderbilt
This place serves Nashville's "Hot Chicken" at its
best. Menu favorites: Chick and Waffle special and
Spicy chicken. Try the root beer float, a perfect
combo with the chicken.

HENRIETTA RED
1200 4th Ave N, Nashville, 615-490-8042
www.henriettared.com
CUISINE: American (New)/Seafood
DRINKS: Full Bar
SERVING: Dinner nightly except Monday, when it's
closed; Lunch Sat & Sun
PRICE RANGE: $$$
NEIGHBORHOOD: Germantown
Communal type eatery with wishbone chairs, a
marble bar, a black sandwich board, offering a menu
of small plates and elevated Gulf seafood from Chef
Julia Sullivan who once worked with the famed
Thomas Keller, but she definitely has her own ideas.
Like the heavenly anchovy butter served with warm
flatbread is worth the visit alone. . Or her roe mixed
with sour cream and spring onions. Oysters (both
coasts are represented) served raw or roasted with
green curry, or stewed with cream and sunchoke. The
snapper tartare is a marvel—ever-so-tender fish set
off with crunchy lavender daikon, cucumber, serrano
chile, toasted nori and crispy quinoa. Squid with fried
polenta is accented with cured lemons and preserved
tomatoes. Lamb sausage highlighted with olives
smoked in a wood-burning hearth that's framed in

tile. Other items I really like are the Cucumber Salad and Baked Ricotta.

HERMITAGE CAFÉ
71 Hermitage Ave, Nashville, 615-254-8871
www.hermitagecafetn.com
CUISINE: American, Diner
DRINKS: No Booze
SERVING: Breakfast, lunch, and late night. Closed for dinner.
PRICE RANGE: $
NEIGHBORHOOD: Downtown
Certainly not to be confused with the grand Hermitage Hotel, this old school diner serves your typical diner cuisine including "breakfast anytime." Menu favorites include: Veggie Omelet and Garden Burger, but I wouldn't eat those—gimme the sausages.

HOG HEAVEN BBQ
115 27th Ave N, Nashville, 615-329-1234
www.hogheavenbbq.com
CUISINE: Barbeque
DRINKS: No Booze
SERVING: Lunch, Early Dinner, Closed Sunday
PRICE RANGE: $
NEIGHBORHOOD: Belmont, Vanderbilt
Located next to Centennial Park, this place is famous for its "Kickin' Chicken" white BBQ sauce. One stop here will demonstrate why this place was featured on Food Network's "Best Thing I Ever Ate." Menu favorites include: Anything BBQ which includes pork, chicken, beef, and turkey. BBQ served in

sandwiches, plates or by the pound. Outdoor seating or take-out.

HONKY TONK CENTRAL
329 Broadway, Nashville, 615-742-9095
www.honkytonkcentral.com
CUISINE: American
DRINKS: Full Bar
SERVING: Lunch, Dinner & Late-night
PRICE RANGE: $$
NEIGHBORHOOD: Downtown
Very busy 3-story pub featuring live music. Menu is typical bar grub like Tattor tots and deep-fried catfish. Huge bar and pub menu. Large TV for sports fans.

HOUSE OF KABOB
216 Thompson Ln, 615-333-3711
http://houseofkabobtn.com/
CUISINE: Persian/Iranian
DRINKS: Full Bar
SERVING: Lunch & Dinner
PRICE RANGE: $$
NEIGHBORHOOD: Woodbine
An eatery with a completely dull interior that happens to have really good food (it better, right?) focusing on kabobs with a selection of chicken, beef, lamb or fish. All served with veggies & rice. Authentic Persian fare like Gyros and Chicken Soltani. Popular take-out eatery.

HUSK

37 Rutledge St, Nashville, 615-256-6565
www.husknashville.com
CUISINE: New Southern
DRINKS: Full Bar
SERVING: Lunch & Dinner daily; weekend Brunch;
indoor-outdoor
PRICE RANGE: $$$
NEIGHBORHOOD: SoBro; Downtown
Just as he did when he made waves internationally in
Charleston, Chef Sean Brock has brought his song
and dance act to Nashville. As the chef puts it, "In
Charleston it's all about the
sea; in Nashville, it's all about the dirt." Led by
Brock, the kitchen explores an ingredient-driven
cuisine that begins in the rediscovery of heirloom
products and redefines what it means to cook and eat
in Nashville. The beautiful red brick building where
Husk is located was built into the side of a hill in the
1880s by Dr. John Bunyan Stephens. Its storied
history includes serving as Mayor Richard Houston

Dudley's home, where he lived when elected in 1897. The area was settled by the Rutledge and Middleton families of Charleston who were descendants of two of the original South Carolina signers of the Declaration of Independence. The design of the Husk's interior spaces enhances the building's roots while demonstrating a sense of Southern style, modernity, energy, and cosmopolitan flair. The classic red brick architecture is enhanced with super high and wide single-pane windows that look outside through the graceful arches on the porch and fill the dining room with light. Menu changes daily. Try the 24-month old country ham with mustard and pickled okra; fried chicken skins served with hot sauce & honey (bring your Lipitor); pimento cheese with Carolina rice cakes; short ribs and beets; shrimp & octopus grits; fried chicken that comes with mac & cheese & cabbage; fried chicken hearts & gizzards; a good bet here if you can visit it more than once is to get the vegetable plate—whatever they have, let them bring it out.

JACKALOPE BREWING COMPANY
701 8th Ave S, Nashville, 615-873-4313
www.jackalopebrew.com
CUISINE: Brewery/Bar Grub
DRINKS: Beer Only
SERVING: Dinner; Lunch & Dinner Sat & Sun
PRICE RANGE: $
NEIGHBORHOOD: The Gulch/Downtown
Cool brewery with a coffee shop attached. A popular hangout with a DJ and plenty of board games. Nice selection of beers and bar menu. Take the tour and

you get a free pint glass plus a few samplings of their beers and a history of the place.

JOSEPHINE
2316 12 Ave S, Nashville, 615-292-7766
www.josephineon12th.com
CUISINE: American
DRINKS: Full Bar
SERVING: Dinner nightly from 5; Friday from 3; brunch on the weekends from 10
PRICE RANGE: $$$
NEIGHBORHOOD: Belmont / Hillsboro / 12 South
An elegant room with dark tufted banquettes against the far wall under a few very large mirrors. Maybe it's the lighting, but the crystal here just seems to "pop." I love the big square bar. Grilled chicken livers with pepper jelly; pickled shrimp; a great selection of fresh veggies; noodles and dumplings; pork jowl served with baby potatoes and pearl onions;

grilled catfish; beef cheeks with a horseradish risotto. As tasty as everything else is, I invariably end up getting the Josephine steak frites with a round dollop of herb butter melting on top of the slices of meat. Dessert? Try the sorghum molasses tart with brown butter. Also the peach shortcake.

KAYNE PRIME
1103 McGavock St, Nashville, 615-259-0050
www.mstreetnashville.com/kayne-prime
CUISINE: American
DRINKS: Full Bar
SERVING: Dinner nightly from 5
PRICE RANGE: $$$$
NEIGHBORHOOD: Downtown; Gulch
Handsome high-back banquettes against the wall. If you sit at the bar, you basically overlook a parking lot, but at night, when Downtown is ablaze with light, it's a different story entirely. 24-ounce bone-in rib eye is spectacular (you can take what you don't eat home); a black kale salad that's much better than it sounds; whole fish of the day grilled or baked; house-made bacon (with a layer of fat on it that makes it

look like a side of pork (I won't even discuss the bacon topped with cotton candy that they serve here—it's scary); broiled trout; mac gratinee that's beyond delicious; duck tacos.

KIEN GIANG
5825 Charlotte Pike, Nashville, 615-353-1250
No Website
CUISINE: Vietnamese
DRINKS: Beer & Wine Only
SERVING: Lunch & Dinner
PRICE RANGE: $ - cash only
Superior Vietnamese specialties in this nothing fancy hole-in-the-wall. The staff may seem brain dead, but I think they're just overworked. Whatever. Whoever is in the kitchen is not brain dead. Get the BBQ pork bahn mi, or the very popular Pho.

LOCKELAND TABLE
1520 Woodland St, Nashville, 615-228-4864
www.lockelandtable.com
CUISINE: American
DRINKS: Full Bar
SERVING: Dinner from 5 (bar opens at 4) except Sunday, when it's closed
PRICE RANGE: $$$
NEIGHBORHOOD: East Nashville
Another one of those unassuming squat brick buildings you see
so often here in Nashville. Inside, however, there's a jumbled design that makes you think they weren't sure what to settle on.

Lights hang from the ceiling amid the industrial look created by the a/c venting. Metal barstools lined up against the curved bar overlooking the kitchen. Somehow it all works beautifully. Smoked Cox Farms bone marrow; pork & shrimp dumplings; chicken liver paté in a jar; hot crispy pig ears; a modest selection of excellent pizzas; rack of lamb; Niman ranch bone-in pork loin; the freshwater trout is particularly good. (Make sure you get a side of the crab & corn fritters.)

THE LOVELESS CAFÉ
8400 Hwy 100, Nashville, 615-646-9700
www.lovelesscafe.com
CUISINE: American; Southern
DRINKS: Full Bar
SERVING: Breakfast, Lunch & Dinner
PRICE RANGE: $$

This is one of those places that's seared in the mind of everybody who grew up in Nashville. This is a "must" stop, even if it is a bit out of town. And yes, the waitresses will call

you, "Honey.") Try to go early or after peak hours because there's usually a waiting line, especially on weekends. And no, it's not just tourists. These are locals. A basket of biscuits comes with every order. It's as Southern as you can get. Everything's made from scratch. You can watch them pull their famous biscuits out of the oven because there's a window into the kitchen. Ham & eggs with red-eye gravy. Ever had a breakfast with pit-cooked BBQ pork and eggs? No? You can here. Steak biscuits (these are very popular) using grilled beef tenderloin; Southern sampler (country ham, bacon, sausage and eggs). If you come for dinner, you'll be just as pleased, however: fried pork chops; grilled catfish; country fried steak; fried chicken livers or gizzards (I used to love these gizzards as a child); homemade meatloaf. All the sides are just perfect, from the fried okra to the mac & cheese. They have an extensive shop and they've been shipping their goods out for decades (now on the Internet). Get gift packs with country ham & bacon; pantry goods; apparel and accessories; gifts; biscuits; preserves; items for the kitchen. Also be sure to check out the **Motel Shops** located in what used to be 14 rooms of the original motel that was behind the café. Stop by to grab some of their jams and preserves to take home.

LYRA
935 W Eastland Ave, 615-928-8040
https://lyranashville.com
CUISINE: Middle Eastern
DRINKS: Full Bar
SERVING: Dinner, Closed Sundays
PRICE RANGE: $$
NEIGHBORHOOD: Greenwood
Casual eatery offering Middle Eastern fare with a modern twist. Favorites: Baba Ghanoush (Stuffed eggplant) and Spiced hanger steak. Vegetarian options. Creative desserts like the Pistachio Ice Cream Sandwich made with a sesame tahini cookie. Nightly Happy hour with nice selection of bites and specialty cocktails.

MARCHÉ ARTISAN FOODS
1000 Main St, Nashville, 615-262-1111
www.marcheartisanfoods.com
CUISINE: Specialty Food
DRINKS: Beer & Wine
SERVING: Breakfast, Lunch & Dinner
PRICE RANGE: $$
NEIGHBORHOOD: East Nashville
Located in historic section of East Nashville, this
European-style café and marketplace offers a
revolving menu. Menu favorites include: Shrimp
Grits and Pan Seared Pork Tenderloin and Cornbread
Panzanella. Breakfast served anytime. Great choice
for weekend brunch.

MARGOT CAFÉ & BAR
1017 Woodland St, Nashville, 615-227-4668
www.margotcafe.com
CUISINE: French, Italian
DRINKS: Full Bar
SERVING: Dinner
PRICE RANGE: $$$
NEIGHBORHOOD: Five Points; East Nashville
This is a special little intimate place, and many people
in-the-know think this is perhaps "the" best restaurant
owned by a chef in the whole of Nashville. (That's
saying something.) Red brick walls with lots of
mirrors hanging on them; wood tables for lunch;
white tablecloths for dinner. Chef Margot earned her
strips in the East Village before returning to Nashville
to work at **F. Scott's** in Green hills. When she opened
this place, she focused on the cuisines she loves most:
southern France and parts of Italy, with an emphasis
on the hearty, healthy peasant cuisines of these

regions. The menu is seasonal and changes every day. Homemade potato chips; Minestra with broccoli pesto; pizza with veal, fava beans and ricotta; pan-roasted redfish; grilled pork chop with squash casserole. (To be honest, this is my first stop for dinner when I get to town.)

MAS TACOS POR FAVOR
732 McFerrin Ave, Nashville, 615-248-4747
No Website
CUISINE: Mexican
DRINKS: No Booze
SERVING: Lunch, Dinner, Closed Sunday
PRICE RANGE: $
NEIGHBORHOOD: East Nashville
This popular "mobile eatery" (I love that term for a food truck) offers a creative menu of tacos and soups. Menu favorites include: Pulled Pork taco and Cast-iron chicken taco. Great place for a fast weekend brunch.

MONELL'S
1235 6th Ave N, Nashville, 615-298-2254
www.MonellsTn.com
CUISINE: Southern; soul food
DRINKS: No Booze
SERVING: Breakfast (from 10), Lunch & Dinner
PRICE RANGE: $$
NEIGHBORHOOD: Germantown
I think the must use a shovel in the kitchen when they
plate the food, there's so much of it. Excellent
Southern food served family style. There's only a
basic menu, with specials every day; Monday,
chicken & dumplings & meatloaf; Tuesday, spinach
lasagna and pot roast; Wednesday, pork chops, baked
chicken and fried chicken (they fry it in a skillet); and
so on and so forth. Full country breakfast available.
Excellent sides like fried apples, cheese grits, corn
pudding. Whatever day it is, it will be good, I
guarantee it.

OTAKU RAMEN
1104 Division St, Nashville, 615-942-8281
www.otakuramen.com
CUISINE: Ramen
DRINKS: Full bar
SERVING: Lunch/Dinner; Closed Mon
PRICE RANGE: $$
NEIGHBORHOOD: The Gulch/Downtown
Trendy eatery offering a menu of traditional ramen
and Japanese fare. Nice selection of ramen – even
vegetarian selections. Try the hot chicken bun
appetizer – delicious.

THE PANCAKE PANTRY
1796 21st Ave S, Nashville, 615-383-9333
www.thepancakepantry.com
CUISINE: Bakeries, Breakfast
DRINKS: No Booze
SERVING: Breakfast & Lunch (6 a.m. to 3 p.m.)
PRICE RANGE: $$
NEIGHBORHOOD: Hillsboro, West End
You'll go crazy for the pancakes here—Swiss
chocolate chip pancakes; especially the sweet potato
pancakes served with a cinnamon syrup. There are
over 20 varieties, like Santa Fe

(cornmeal pancakes with bits of bacon, cheddar and
green chilis), the Caribbean (buttermilk cakes with
pecans, coconut, powdered sugar, slices of banana).
It's hard to get a seat at one of the Formica tables
here. The lines are very long, so plan on going early
or late at off peak hours. There's plenty more on the
menu if you're not eating carbs: sandwiches; burgers;
ham and egg plates, lots more.

PENINSULA
1035 W Eastland Ave, 615-679-0377
www.peninsulanashville.com
CUISINE: Portuguese/Spanish
DRINKS: Full Bar
SERVING: Dinner, Closed Sun & Mon.
PRICE RANGE: $$
NEIGHBORHOOD: East Nashville
Modern eatery offering the cuisines of Iberia. They
had to add a few beams to the ceiling here in an effort
to create a little atmosphere. High wide windows
looking out to the residential neighborhood across the
street are nice, bringing in lots of light. The place is
simple, and just fine. The focus here is the quality of
the Spanish and Portuguese dishes they offer, and
they couldn't be better. Not what you expect here in
Nashville. Favorites: Chick gizzards passion fruit,
turmeric; Morcilla Crepe with sweetbreads and onion
(very nice); Braised rabbit (this is a dish they are
justifiably very proud of) with garlic broth &
pimenton. Main courses: Pork Cheeks with Squid
Ink. Interesting desserts. Impressive wine list.

PEPPERFIRE HOT CHICKEN
1000 Gallatin Ave, Nashville, 615-582-4824
www.pepperfirechicken.com
CUISINE: Southern, Comfort Food
DRINKS: No Booze
SERVING: Lunch, Dinner; closed Sunday
PRICE RANGE: $
NEIGHBORHOOD: Gallatin Pike

This is a carry–out eatery only but there are picnic tables in front those too hungry to wait until they get home. The menu is a variety of chicken dishes and sandwiches—the deep-fried grilled cheese sandwich is well worth trying.

PHARMACY BURGER PARLOR AND BEER GARDEN
731 McFerrin, Nashville, 615-712-9517
www.thepharmacynashville.com
CUISINE: American; Burgers; pub fare
DRINKS: Beer & Wine
SERVING: Lunch & Dinner daily
PRICE RANGE: $$
NEIGHBORHOOD: East Nashville
Just a square white building from the outside, but inside there's a good vibe where locals meet to eat fantastic burgers and drink beer. Has an impressive selection of German wurst and German beer. There's a Stroganoff Burger (mushroom stroganoff béchamel,

sour cream, caramelized onion, Swiss cheese); among many others, as well as lots of German wursts: Jagerwurst, Bratwurst, Currywurst, Bauerwurst, Kielbasa, Bockwurst. Sides are handmade and uniformly excellent. Also there's an old-school sofa fountain serving up phosphates, milkshakes and ice cream sodas. In good weather, sit in the beer garden out back under the string of lights criss-crossing above you in the leafy canopy. (The ice cream here is particularly good.)

PRINCE'S HOT CHICKEN SHACK
5814 Nolensville Pike, Nashville, 615-810-9388
https://princeshotchicken.com
CUISINE: Southern
DRINKS: No Booze
SERVING: Lunch, Dinner; closed Sunday
PRICE RANGE: $
Known as the pioneer of Hot Chicken, this place serves a variety of Hot Chicken in pieces, strips or whole. It's quite popular so expect a wait. The story goes that back in the 1930s, Thornton Prince came home very late after cheating on his girlfriend. To get back at him, she gave him fried chicken loaded down with cayenne pepper. Her trick backfired, because he loved it. He even opened the country's first "hot chicken" place in the mid-1930s. If you can handle the heat, you'll find the chicken they fry is moist and juicy inside. They will warn you not to touch your eyes after eating this chicken.

PUCKETT'S GROCERY & RESTAURANT
www.puckettsgrocery.com

CUISINE: American
DRINKS: Full Bar
SERVING: Breakfast, Lunch, Dinner daily
PRICE RANGE: $$
NEIGHBORHOOD: Downtown
Great location in a corner building in Downtown. Not only is it a good restaurant, but there's a store and live music as well on the little stage on one side of the dining room. Ultra-casual atmosphere. Your drinks come in mason jars. Pulled pork sliders; fried pickles & jalapenos; fried green tomatoes & chipotle dip; cherry-smoked hot wings; Southern fried catfish; Piggy Mac (smoked pulled pork in an iron skillet topped with smoked gouda mac & cheese); smoked baby back ribs. (Get the Maple Pecan Pie if you can manage it after stuffing yourself with all this comfort food.) If you're here for breakfast, try the Bubba's Eggs Benedict (split biscuits topped with bacon or sausage covered with 2 fried eggs and smothered in pepper gravy).

ROLF AND DAUGHTERS
700 Taylor St, Nashville, 615-866-9897
www.rolfanddaughters.com
CUISINE: American, Mediterranean
DRINKS: Full Bar
SERVING: Dinner
PRICE RANGE: $$$
NEIGHBORHOOD: Germantown
This restaurant, run by Chef Philip Krajeck, offers a
beautiful dining experience in a refurbished Werthan
packaging factory that's a century old. It has brick
walls, old slats of reclaimed wood on the high ceiling
above and these tall wide windows with no drapes or
anything that gives it a workhouse look. At the long
dorm style common table stretching down the center,
you almost expect to see Oliver Twist eating his
gruel. A great atmosphere. The Belgian-raised Chef

Krajeck is famous around these parts not for his gruel, but for his fresh pasta. Among the more unique eateries in town, Rolf combines Southern food with a Northern Italian - Mediterranean twist. Menu favorites include: Crispy-Skinned Chicken; Pork Tenderloin; chicken-liver pate served with a green tomato jam; meatballs and dandelion greens.

SILO
1121 5th Ave N, Nashville, 615-750-2912
www.silotn.com
CUISINE: Southern; bistro
DRINKS: Full Bar
SERVING: Dinner daily at 5; bar opens at 4 for happy hour; Sunday brunch from 10:30
PRICE RANGE: $$
NEIGHBORHOOD: Germantown
A simple red brick building with floor-to-ceiling windows looking outside. Inside, it's wood, wood, wood, from the tables to the chairs to the walls. The tables were made by a local artisan from Ethridge, Tennessee. The pendant lights came from another artist in Louisville. The space features a community table, a private dining room, a large bar area, two patios and an open kitchen. One of the owners came from the French Culinary Institute and the other one from a bakery in Charleston, so you have a heady mix of Southern food with French bistro twists. Smokey pork spare ribs with a Coco Cola BBQ sauce; baby beets and sautéed kale; cast iron scallion-jalapeno cornbread; chicken confit; hangar steak. If you come for Sunday Brunch, get the pulled pork eggs Benedict

style with a jalapeno hollandaise to create a nice bite that'll wake you right up.

SKULL'S RAINBOW ROOM
222 Printers Alley, Nashville, 615-810-9631
www.skullsrainbowroom.com
CUISINE: Modern American
DRINKS: Full bar
SERVING: Lunch/Dinner
PRICE RANGE: $$
NEIGHBORHOOD: Downtown
Located in historic Printers Alley, this eatery offers a menu of American fare, crafted cocktails and live burlesque shows (twice nightly). Menu favorites: Grilled salmon and Lobster bisque. Reservations recommended.

SOUTHERN STEAK & OYSTER
150 3ʳᵈ Ave S, Nashville, 615-724-1762

www.thesouthernnashville.com
CUISINE: American; New Southern
DRINKS: Full Bar
SERVING: Breakfast weekdays from 7:30; Lunch
daily; Dinner nightly (but bar opens for happy hour at
3); brunch on weekends from 10 am
PRICE RANGE: $$$
NEIGHBORHOOD: Downtown; SoBro
Has a very New York feel with its subway style
bathroom white-tiled floor, expansive back bar and
thin-strips of wood in the ceiling. This is a very good
place for breakfast: Southern omelet (braised pork,
onions, collards, black-eyes peas, cheddar, served
with grits or potatoes); smoked brisket with jalapeno
cheddar grits and 2 fried eggs; or the fried egg
sandwich. Later on, I like the daily selection of
oysters. They usually have two or 3 types. Also the
Dominican braised pork; bahn mi tacos; double-cut
smoked pork chop; baby back ribs; dry aged strip
steak.

TAVERN

1904 Broadway, Nashville, 615-320-8580
www.mstreetnashville.com/tavern/
CUISINE: Gastro pub; some Asian; some Mexican
DRINKS: Full Bar
SERVING: Lunch and Dinner daily; Brunch on weekends from 10 am; open till 3 am Friday & Saturday
PRICE RANGE: $$ to $$$
NEIGHBORHOOD: Downtown
Wraparound booths create a cozy atmosphere within the lively bar scene in this high-ceilinged room. A half-raised mezzanine level lets you look down on the bar scene while you eat. Later in the evening, they shift to more energetic beat, with DJs cranking out the tunes. (They stay open till about 3 am on Friday and Saturday.) Lots of TVs for the sports-inclined. Has

one of the better brunches on weekends. Small plates like wood-grilled artichokes; egg rolls; fried chicken skins; chili scallops. A great selection of creative tacos: fish, lamb, chicken, short ribs. Also an impressive line-up of salads and sandwiches; mahi, tuna salad, lobster sliders, patak bratwurst, as well as a great burger. Main plates include grilled hamburger steak with a fried egg on top; a basket of crispy little fish (cornmeal fried catfish); lots of specialty cocktails. If you're here for brunch, get the White Trash Hash and the Benedict Uno with braised short ribs. The brunches are very busy.

TENNESSEE BREW WORKS
809 Ewing Ave, Nashville, 615-436-0050
www.tnbrew.com
CUISINE: Brewery/Burgers
DRINKS: Beer & Wine Only
SERVING: Lunch/Dinner
PRICE RANGE: $$
NEIGHBORHOOD: Downtown
Basically a brewery serving beers brewed on-site but if you're hungry you can order a burger. Tours available for a small fee. Lots of games to keep the drinkers occupied. Raves for the burgers and beers.

TWO TEN JACK
1900 Eastland Ave #105, Nashville, 615-454-2731
www.twotenjack.com
CUISINE: Ramen
DRINKS: Full Bar
SERVING: Dinner, closed Sun
PRICE RANGE: $$

NEIGHBORHOOD: Lockeland Springs
A Japanese-inspired neighborhood pub that offers a menu of kodawari ramen, skewers & grilled items, sushi and Japanese inspired pub comfort food. Handcrafted cocktails.

VIRAGO
1120 McGavock St, Nashville, 615-254-1902
www.mstreetnashville.com/virago
CUISINE: Japanese; robata grill & sushi bar
DRINKS: Full Bar
SERVING: Dinner nightly from 5
PRICE RANGE: $$$
NEIGHBORHOOD: Downtown; Gulch
Has a strikingly modern design inside with a slanted ceiling held up by stark metal posts; wood and brick, recessed lighting. Lobster tacos; crispy Brussels sprouts; Tsukune chicken meatballs; bacon wrapped scallops; Mune chicken breast; smoked brisket Udon; tuffled black grouper; salt & pepper shrimp. There's a very nice rooftop bar with a view of Downtown, so go up there if you can.

WHISKEY KITCHEN
118 12th Ave S, Nashville, 615-254-3029
www.mstreetnashville.com
CUISINE: American (New)
DRINKS: Full Bar
SERVING: Lunch, Dinner
PRICE RANGE: $$
NEIGHBORHOOD: Downtown

Popular bar with a menu of tavern grub. Menu favorites include: Blackbean burger, Braised beef short ribs and Whiskey brownie cheesecake.

ZOLLIKOFFE
701 8th Ave S, Nashville, 615-873-4315
www.zollikoffee.com
CUISINE: Bakery/Sandwiches
DRINKS: No Booze
SERVING: Breakfast, Lunch & Early Dinner
PRICE RANGE: $$
NEIGHBORHOOD: Downtown
Located inside the **Jackalope Brewing Company**, a coffee shop serving up a menu of healthy breakfast and baked goods. Menu features variety of sandwiches and sweets like the popular dark chocolate cake with almonds. Excellent coffee.

Chapter 4
NIGHTLIFE

THE 5 SPOT
1006 Forrest Ave., Nashville, 615-650-9333
http://the5spotlive.com/blog/
NEIGHBORHOOD: East Nashville, near Five Points
This long narrow bar with a stage at the far end is a
great spot for dancing, cheap beer, lots of live music,
offering up multiple acts every night except Monday.
There's a modest menu offering a couple of pizzas
and some sandwiches if you want a snack. They have
a gay dance party on the third Friday of every month
called **QDP (Queer Dance Party).**

THE BASEMENT
917 Woodland St, Nashville, 615-645-9174
www.thebasementnashville.com
This small venue books a wide variety of music acts, from country singer to indie bands. Check the web site for schedule. No smoking inside. 21 and over. If you go upstairs, you'll find one of the best indie record stores in town (maybe even the country), **Grimey's New & Preloved Music.**

BASTION
434 Houston St, Nashville, 615-490-8434
www.bastionnashville.com
NEIGHBORHOOD: South Nashville, Wedgewood-Houston
This little warehouse-style bar, connected to the restaurant, is right out of a trailer park, very low-brow but don't let its looks fool you—they serve up highly creative cocktails, as well as draft beer and wine. They have nachos if you need a snack. Their Punch of the Day changes every day, so give it a try.

BEARDED IRIS BREWING TAPROOM
101 Van Buren St, Nashville, 615-928-7988
www.beardedirisbrewing.com
NEIGHBORHOOD: East Germantown
Brewery taproom serving rotating selection of old-world style beer. Comfortable atmosphere with velvet couches, large chandelier and an old pool table. Known for their IPA (India Pale Ale). Usually there's a food truck parked outside that serves up very tasty food if you're hungry.

BLUEBIRD CAFÉ
4104 Hillsboro Pike, Nashville, 615-383-1461
www.bluebirdcafe.com
If you're a singer or a songwriter, performing here is like a "coming of age" experience. They usually have 2 shows a night. The cozy (OK, tight and crowded) room that seats only 100 lucky customers is actually a good thing, not a bad thing. You feel like you're seeing tomorrow's stars, and in many cases, you really are. If you're a fan of the show "Nashville," you've seen what you think is this place on TV. Though they perform on a set (accurate even down to the line of lights strung along the bar), it's uncanny how well they captured this place. The walls are plastered with pictures of some of the thousands of musicians who've performed here. You'll want to reserve a seat, but reservations open usually Monday at 8 a.m. for the shows that week. They go fast. They serve food, but it's not that good, so eat elsewhere and come here for the show. Plan on showing up early. They will give your reserved seat to someone else if you're a minute late.

BOBBY'S IDLE HOUR
1028 16th Ave S, Nashville, 615-726-0446
www.bobbysidlehour.com
A dive bar with live music. Wednesday and Thursday night jams. A favorite hangout of local songwriters. People on the way up in the music business gather here, as well as people on the way down.

BONGO JAVA
2007 Belmont Blvd, Nashville, 615-385-5282
www.bongojava.com
NEIGHBORHOOD: Belmont, Hillsboro
Right across the street from Belmont University is
this place that's a hangout for lots of artists, students,
musicians and those who want to be around them.
You can mix and mingle with them over a cup of
coffee or a snack. Try the Juanita Burrita (3 eggs,
grilled onions & jalapenos with chipotle cream cheese
& jack cheese in a tortilla—comes with hashbrowns
and house salsa). They also have burgers, several
sandwiches, tacos, grilled cheese, salads. Above the
coffeeshop is the **Bongo After Hours Theatre**,
which showcases theatre, musical events, improve,
classes and workshops.

BUTCHERTOWN HALL
1416 4th Ave N, Nashville, 615-454-3634
www.butchertownhall.com
NEIGHBORHOOD: Germantown
Rustic-chic hall that serves incredible cocktails and
brews. Some come to drink, others to eat – nice
selection of Mexican-inspired eats like tacos and
queso. But the beer is the star attraction here, though
there are some nicely prices good wines as well.

CHAUHAN ALE & MASALA HOUSE
123 12th Ave N, Nashville, 615-242-8426
www.chauhannashville.com
NEIGHBORHOOD: Downtown

Located in a refurbished brick garage, this place offers a menu of creative Indian fare and exceptional cocktails. Bar offers a worldwide selection of wine and spirits and crafted cocktails.

CRYING WOLF
823 Woodland St, Nashville, 615-953-6715
www.thecryingwolf.com
A no-frills bar that also serves burgers.

EAST NASHVILLE
Across the Cumberland River is the hippest area of town called East Nashville. This is where the more cutting edge segment of the population lives and works and hangs out (the artists, the musicians, etc.), and you'd be doing yourself a disservice if you don't venture over here. It's East Nashville that's giving the town its international press, not Downtown. Just as in any other town where these people congregate, the restaurants, coffeehouses, cafes, nightclubs, lounges and shops have sprouted up to serve their needs.

DOUGLAS CORNER CAFÉ
2106A 8th Ave S, Nashville, 615-298-1688
www.douglascorner.com
NEIGHBORHOOD: 12 South
You can experience real country music here, whether it's a local act or a touring group. Every month (on the last Wednesday), a group called **45rpm** offers up traditional country music. Not to be missed.

THE END
2219 Elliston Pl, Nashville, 615-321-4457

www.endnashville.com
This is another great venue where you can hear
excellent indie rock bands, both local and national.

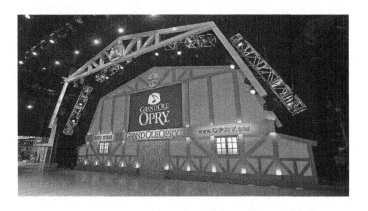

GRAND OLE OPRY HOUSE
2804 Opryland Drive, Nashville, 615-871-6779
www.opry.com
The live-performance radio program that put
Nashville on the map is still going strong, even after
the horrendous 2010 flood that wrecked the building.
All is well, however, in the refurbished venue. Even if
you HATE country music, you've got to make an
effort to squeeze this into your itinerary. There's a
backstage tour of the facility. You'll be able to stand
onstage where thousands of legendary performers
have stood "in the circle." You'll learn the history of
the Opry (it started at the Ryman Auditorium
downtown) and how it developed, and all of it is very
interesting. You'll get to see the old studio where
"Hee Haw" was filmed, and you'll get to see a show
running a couple of hours featuring a steady stream of
entertainers, comedians, singers. This will likely be

the standout experience of your visit if you make the plunge and do it. It's something you'll never forget as long as you live.

THE HIGH WATT
1 Cannery Row, Nashville, 615-251-3020
www.mercylounge.com
A cozy little club housed in a century-old former cannery showcases local up and coming bands and national talents. 500 capacity music venue with a back bar that features pool tables and booth seating.

HONKEY TONK CENTRAL
329 Broadway, Nashville, 615-742-9095
www.honkytonkcentral.com
Very busy 3-story pub featuring live music. Huge bar and pub menu. Large TV for sports fans. It's a big-time tourist trap.

HURRY BACK
2212 Elliston Pl, Nashville, 615-915-0764
www.hurry-back.com
Great selection of rare and craft beers. Bar fare menu. TVs and big projector for sports. Outdoor seating.

MELROSE BILLIARDS
2600 8th Ave S, Nashville, 615-678-5489
www.dirtymelrose.com
This is a true dive bar filled with lots of old-time regulars. Cheap prices, pool tables, ping pong, and snooker. Everybody from construction workers to studio musicians.

NO. 308
407 Gallatin Ave, Nashville, 615-650-7344
www.bar308.com/
Trendy late-night hangout serving craft cocktails.
Patio seating and popular happy hour. (Get the 308
sliders if you're hungry.)

OAK BAR
THE HERMITAGE HOTEL
231 Sixth Ave N, Nashville, 615-345-7116
http://www.capitolgrillenashville.com/oak-bar.asp
NEIGHBORHOOD: Downtown; Lower Broadway
Though I'm putting this in the nightlife chapter, it's
also a perfect place to meet for a drink before dinner,
or to come when winding down the evening for a
Cognac after dinner or a show. Opens at 11:30 for
drinks and also has a casual menu (fried pickles;
smoked bologna sandwich; Granny's deviled eggs;
hunter's plate of house-cured smoked meats and
pickled items; Brunswick stew; BBQ shrimp; the
Tennessee Stack is two 4-ounce Double H beef
patties with cheddar, pepper jelly, sweet onion and
hot mustard), and is open for happy hour from 4:30 to
6:30.

PINEWOOD SOCIAL
33 Peabody St, Nashville, 615-751-8111
www.pinewoodsocial.com
Trendy industrial-chic hangout open all day. The
location used to be a trolley car depot, so it has a
funky charm. The place is divided into three parts—
couches in the front section are nice for a cup of
Crema coffee in the morning; the middle section is

great for innovative cocktails and some food (the catfish sandwich is my favorite); the section in the back is where they have vintage bowling lanes and karaoke. In the summer, there's even a pool on the patio.

THE PATTERSON HOUSE
1711 Division St, Nashville, 615-636-7724
www.thepattersonnashville.com
This dark, luxurious bar throwing off a speakeasy vibe and sporting vintage chandeliers and rows of bookshelves serves delicious old-fashioned cocktails late into the night. There's a velvet curtain you pass through, a bar in the center with stools and a series of booths against the walls lit by candles. They are very

serious about the craft cocktails served here, down to the point that they make their own bitters in house. Bacon Old Fashioned has maple syrup in it; the classic Sidecar is served, one of my favorite drinks. The small plate menu items are all made to order, from the potato chips to the truffled deviled eggs; beef sliders & tater tots; cinnamon sugar donuts; fig & prosciutto flatbread (and don't overlook the donut holes). One of my all-time favorite places in Nashville.

ROBERT'S WESTERN WORLD
416B Broadway, Nashville, 615-244-9552
www.robertswesternworld.com
NEIGHBORHOOD: Downtown
In Nashville, when you say you're going "honky-tonking," it means you're going out on the town. This

is one of the best places to do that. A super variety of great musical acts fills their schedule. You can't miss their big sign right on Broadway with the lit up guitar. Also has good white trash food: fried Bolonga sandwiches, grilled cheese, cheap burgers that are so juicy and flavorful, really good hot dogs. I don't know anybody who doesn't absolutely love this place. When it's really crowded on Friday and Saturday nights, go to the back-alley entrance next to the Ryman Auditorium where you'll find a doorman who's checking IDs, but you can still get in with less hassle.

SANTA'S PUB
2225 Bransford Ave, Nashville, 615-593-1872
www.santaspub.com
Busy dive bar located in a triple-wide trailer. Holiday décor all year with cheap beer and karaoke that seems to be continuous. You can miss the mural of the Santa on the motorcycle on the front of the building. Cash only.

SPRINGWATER
115 27th Ave N, Nashville, 615-320-0345
www.springwatersupperclub.com
My younger readers won't know who he is, but Jimmy Hoffa used to hang out here in one of the best beer-only dive bars in Nashville that once-upon-a-time was a speakeasy. It's located next to Centennial Park. You'll encounter a bunch of drunks spending their Social Security checks, college kids looking to slum it. But the jukebox is good and they have arcade games.

THE STAGE ON BROADWAY
412 Broadway, Nashville, 615-726-0504
www.thestageonbroadway.com
A Honky-Tonk that mixes the flavor of Texas with
Nashville. Live country music and a dance floor.
Never a cover charge. Country music for people
wearing flip flops.

STATION INN
402 12th Ave S, Nashville, 615-255-3307
www.stationinn.com
NEIGHBORHOOD: Downtown; Gulch
When you first get a glimpse of this plain concrete
building, you get the sense that this place doesn't
really belong here because the Gulch area has become
so trendy, with expensive new condos rising around
it. But this is one of the top destinations in town
because of its excellent bluegrass and old-time shows

that continue to attract crowds, as they have for many years. Every time I go there, I hear brilliant music, especially bluegrass and Western swing. On any given night, while you down your Bud Light and eat popcorn, you might see Ronnie Bowman, Guy Clark or another, younger player everyone's going to be talking about in a couple years.

THE SUTLER SALOON
2600 Franklin Pike, Nashville, 615-840-6124
www.thesutler.com
Rustic-chic late-night hangout serving craft cocktails and Southern fare. Live music.

TOOTSIE'S ORCHID LOUNGE
422 Broadway, Nashville, 615-726-0463
www.tootsies.net/
One of Nashville's original Honky Tonks. The place is filled with memories and photos of bands that have played there. Great place to hang out and watch the

locals mingle with the musicians who fill the place. Willie Nelson grew up signing here and Patsy Cline used to drink here. Kristofferson used to hang out here as well.

WHISKEY KITCHEN
118 12th Ave S, Nashville, 615-254-3029
www.mstreetnashville.com
Busy and welcoming watering hole featuring a menu of global whiskeys and tavern fare. This is a good place to begin your tour of the area's nightlife opportunities.

Chapter 5
WHAT TO SEE & DO

ADVENTURE SCIENCE CENTER
800 Fort Negley Blvd, Nashville, 615-862-5160
www.adventuresci.org
This institution seeks to inspire curiosity in all things
scientific, and to encourage a lifelong discovery of
science. They've been here since 1945. With 44,000
square feet of exhibit space, the Center features
nearly 200 hands-on exhibits focused on biology,

physics, visual perception, listening, mind, air and
space, energy and earth science. A great place to
bring the kids, though I go all by myself. Their
award-winning programs include daily science
demonstrations, Discovery Cart activities, workshops,
lectures, camps, Science Cafes and other special
events. The **Sudekum Planetarium** features state-of-
the-art digital projection and surround sound to
present programs on a wide range of sciences, history,
culture and laser shows.

BELLE MEADE PLANTATION
110 Leake Ave, Nashville, 615-356-0501
www.bellemeadeplantation.com
There's an ancient log cabin on the grounds of this
beautiful old plantation that dates back to 1790, but
more interesting is the plantation itself that dates back
to 1853 (the carriage house was added in 1890).
Guided tours are filled with interesting historical
information. Modest fee.

BELMONT MANSION
1700 Acklen Ave, Nashville, 615-460-5459

www.belmontmansion.com

NEIGHBORHOOD: Belmont, Hillsboro

This is one of the top attractions in town, and is the biggest "house museum" in Tennessee. The moving spirit behind Belmont Mansion is Adelicia Hayes Franklin Acklen Cheatham. She was born on 1817,into a prominent Nashville family. At the age of 22, Adelicia married her first husband, Isaac Franklin, a wealthy businessman and plantation owner who was 28 years her senior. They had four children, all of whom died before the age of 11. After seven years of marriage, Isaac Franklin died unexpectedly of a stomach virus while visiting one of his plantations in Louisiana. Adelicia inherited a huge estate including: 8,700 acres of cotton plantations in Louisiana; Fairvue, a 2,000-acre farm in Tennessee; more than 50,000 acres of undeveloped land in Texas; stocks and bonds; and 750 slaves. In 1846, at the age of 29, Adelicia Franklin was independently wealthy, worth about $1 million. In 1849, she remarried, to Joseph Alexander Smith Acklen, a Mexican War hero and a lawyer from Huntsville, Alabama. Together they built Belmont Mansion (originally named Belle Monte), completing construction in 1853. You'll definitely want to take the guided tour of the 16 rooms on the tour.

BICENTENNIAL CAPITOL MALL STATE PARK

600 James Robertson Pkwy, Nashville, 615-741-5280
http://tnstateparks.com/parks/about/bicentennial-mall
NEIGHBORHOOD: Downtown

In this park laid out before the Capitol you'll see a huge 200-foot large granite map of Tennessee, but it offers other features that make it the No. 1 attraction in all of Nashville: the farmers' market, the fish market, a nursery, fountains where you'll see kids playing, a large WW II memorial, a 95-bell Carillon, the Pathway of History and the Rivers of Tennessee Fountains. The 11 planters along the Walkway of Counties show native plant species from different regions of the state. The two-page park map is a helpful and informative tool for those wishing to take a self-guided tour of the park. Park rangers provide interpretive park tours, historical presentations in period dress and off-site programs by reservation. Program topics illustrate Tennessee's rich history from early settlement days to present time. To schedule an interpretive tour, presentation or off-site program, you can call 615-741-5771.

CARNTON PLANTATION
1345 Eastern Flank Circle, Nashville, 615-794-0903
www.carnton.org
On the site of this plantation there was a big Civil War confrontation between the Unikon and confederate armies known as the Battle of Franklin. You can take a comprehensive walking tour of this battlefield. Tour guides focus on many elements of the Battle of Franklin, explaining why it occurred, the arrival of the Federal and Confederate armies, and the details of what became known as one of the greatest single assaults of the Civil War. (There is a fee.) Battlefield Tours are offered Tuesday through Friday at 11 A.M. Reservations are encouraged, but not

required. Carnton was built in 1826 by former Nashville mayor Randal McGavock (1768-1843). Throughout the nineteenth century it was frequently visited by those shaping Tennessee and American history, including President Andrew Jackson. Carnton grew to become one of the premier farms in Williamson County. Beginning at 4 p.m. on November 30, 1864, Carnton was witness to one of the bloodiest battles of the entire Civil War. Everything the McGavock family ever knew was forever changed. The Confederate Army of Tennessee furiously assaulted the Federal army entrenched along the southern edge of Franklin. The resulting battle, believed to be the bloodiest five hours of the Civil War, involved a massive frontal assault larger than Pickett's Charge at Gettysburg. The majority of the combat occurred in the dark and at close quarters. The Battle of Franklin lasted barely five hours and led to some 9,500 soldiers being killed, wounded, captured, or counted as missing. Nearly 7,000 of that number were Confederate troops. Carnton served as the largest field hospital in the area for hundreds of wounded and dying Confederate soldiers. A staff officer later wrote that "the wounded, in hundreds, were brought to [the house] during the battle, and all the night after. And when the noble old house could hold no more, the yard was appropriated until the wounded and dead filled that...." On the morning of December 1, 1864 the bodies of four Confederate generals killed during the fighting, Patrick R. Cleburne, Hiram B. Granbury, John Adams, and Otho F. Strahl, lay on Carnton's back porch. The floors of the restored home are still stained with the blood of the men who were treated here, and you can see these stains.

COUNTRY MUSIC HALL OF FAME & MUSEUM

222 5th Ave S, Nashville, 615-416-2001
www.countrymusichalloffame.org
NEIGHBORHOOD: Downtown
They have doubled the original size of this museum and added lots more exhibits. The tours here are all self-guided. WSM radio personality Bill Cody takes you on a tour through the different eras of country music and his narrative provides behind the scenes stories, insider tips, personal memories and more. With the newly expanded exhibit space, they suggest allowing approximately 2-3 hours to experience the museum. However, depending upon your own pace or if you decide to participate in any of their programs, you may like to stay longer. Your ticket is good all day, so you may come and go as needed. There's so much for you to explore. You can see Bill Monroe's mandolin, Elvis Presley's shiny Cadillac, tacky as all get-out with its ground-up pearls, diamonds and fish scales. Oh, and hundreds of

guitars. Aside from the Museum and Hall of Fame, they also offer tours of **Historic RCA Studio B** (Nashville's only historic studio tour) and **Hatch Show Print** (one of America's oldest letterpress print shops). Allow approximately an hour for each tour. Shop in one of four retail stores and have lunch or a snack in their full-service restaurant, **Two Twenty-Two Grill.**

FAIRGROUNDS SPEEDWAY
625 Smith Ave, Nashville, 615-254-1986
www.fairgroundsspeedwaynashville.com/
Located on the Tennessee State Fairgrounds, this is the second oldest continually operating track in the United States.

FRIST CENTER FOR THE VISUAL ARTS
919 Broadway, Nashville, 615-244-3340
www.fristcenter.org
NEIGHBORHOOD: Downtown

The Frist Center opened in April 2001 (in a gorgeous Art Deco building that once housed the post office), and since that time has hosted a spectacular array of art from the region, the country, and around the world. It's become a magnet for Nashville's rapidly expanding visual arts scene. With an exhibitions schedule that has new art flowing through the magnificent Art Deco building every 6 to 8 weeks, no matter how often you visit, there is always something new and exciting to see in the spacious galleries. The Frist Center was conceived as a family-friendly place and one of the most popular locations in the center is the innovative **Martin ArtQuest Gallery**. With 30 interactive stations, and the assistance of knowledgeable staff and volunteers, ArtQuest teaches through activity. Make a print, paint your own original watercolor, create your own colorful sculpture. It's all there in ArtQuest, and it's free with gallery admission for adults and always free for youth 18 and under. While at the Frist Center, be sure to stop by the **Gift Shop**. There, you'll find a fabulous array of art prints, books, educational materials, art supplies, clothing, blown glass, pottery, and magnificent jewelry made by local and regional artisans. Items are available in a wide range of prices, so there's always something to fit your budget. Because much of the merchandise relates to the Frist Center's exhibitions, the selection changes often. (It might even be the best gift shop in Nashville. The popular Frist Center **Café** features a variety of homemade soups, desserts, salads, and sandwiches, making the Café a popular gathering place for brunch, lunch, afternoon snacks, and dinner on Thursday and

Friday evenings when the Frist Center stays open until 9 p.m.

GENERAL JACKSON SHOWBOAT
2812 Opryland Drive, Nashville, 615-458-3900
www.generaljackson.com
This 300-foot-long paddlewheel boat offers Midday Cruises, Sunday Brunch and Evening Cruises, including buffet and show. It's the only thing like it in Nashville. After the meal on the Midday Cruise, you get a country music variety show, **Nashville Live**. The world-class cast includes two rising country artists, an internationally acclaimed trick-roper, a country comedian and features fiddle and guitar soloists, all supported by a live country band. The show's repertoire spans classic hits by Patsy Cline, George Jones and Tammy Wynette through today's chart-topping hits by Jason Aldean, Taylor Swift and Rascal Flatts. The Evening Cruise offers the same

great views of downtown Nashville and followed by the show, from bluegrass to soul, a little gospel and, of course, country music. Covering classic Elvis to the new artists of country music, the cast of seven is backed by a live six-piece band. The Sunday Brunch Cruise you get a Southern buffet, and afterwards, a vocal quartet and three instrumentalists singing "Down by the Riverside," "Good Ole Gospel Ship," "Get All Excited" and other traditional Southern Gospel favorites and contemporary Christian music with songs like "Your Grace is Enough" and "I Could Sing of Your Love Forever."

HELISTAR AVIATION
220 Tune Airport Drive, Nashville, 615-350-1122
www.flyhelistar.com
Helicopter tours.

THE HERMITAGE

4580 Rachels Lane, Nashville, 615-889-2941
www.thehermitage.com

Constructed from 1819 to 1821 by skilled carpenters
and masons from the local area, the original section of
the Hermitage mansion was a brick Federal-style
house. This design was a typical plantation dwelling
for aspiring gentleman farmers in the Upper South but
was already beginning to lose favor in more
fashionable Eastern areas. The house contained eight
rooms–four on each floor–and two wide center halls.
This symmetrical center hall style plan held its
popularity in the South for many years, and in fact
was used in my Godparents' house, Marston
Plantation, in Stateburg, S.C., so when I first walked

in here, I felt right at home. The first floor contained two parlors, a dining room, and Andrew and Rachel Jackson's bedroom. The upstairs held four bedrooms. The elegant house featured a basement summer kitchen, nine fireplaces, an entrance fanlight, French wallpaper, and metal gutters. Later, Jackson added a small plain entrance portico.

In 1831, while Jackson was President, he undertook a major remodeling directed by architect David Morrison. Morrison dramatically renovated the mansion with flanking one-story wings, a two-story entrance portico with ten Doric columns, a small rear portico, and copper gutters. The east wing contained a library and farm office while a large dining room and pantry comprised the west wing. A new kitchen and smokehouse were also built behind the 13-room mansion. Morrison's remodeling gave the house a new Classical appearance. Lots of Jackson's possessions are on display. The mansion is surrounded by extensive grounds. There's a great gift shop here, too.

HONKY TONK HIGHWAY

Bars and clubs are called "honky tonks" here in Nashville. Broadway in Downtown is where you want to be. There's a never-ending series of bars that provide a wide range of live music. You'll encounter even more musicians out on the sidewalks earning their keep from tips from people like you passing by. Neon signs line the whole street, giving the place an other-worldly glow. The TV show "Nashville" has filmed inside some of the bars, including **Layla's Bluegrass Inn** and **Tootsie's Orchid Lounge**. Tootsie's, which opened in 1960, is the top dog on the Honky Tonk Highway. Country artists such as Kris Kristofferson and Willie Nelson played there when they were young.

photo by
karen timberman

NATIONAL ZOO AT GRASSMERE
3777 Nolensville Pike, Nashville, 615-833-1534
www.nashvillezoo.org
This is not just a zoo, but really more like an
amusement park, it has so many things to do. You can
visit the **CROFT HOME**, built in 1810—it's the
centerpiece of the **GRASSMERE HISTORIC
FARM** and is open seasonally for guided tours.
Guides will take you on a walking tour through the
home, telling you the history of the property, stories
from the five generations who lived there, and how
the Zoo came to be located on the land. During the
tour, you will see many original pieces of furniture, a
portion of the extensive book collection, and several
family portraits. Be sure to look for the name that was
etched on a pane of glass over 100 years ago. After
touring the home, you can explore the rest of the farm
grounds, including the three-tier heirloom garden and

the family cemetery, which is the final resting place for several family members. You will really want to see **THE CASSOWARY EXHIBIT**. The cassowary is a keystone species to Australia and New Guinea playing a vital role in the growth of the rainforest. Known as the Gardener of the Rainforest, cassowaries can germinate more than 200 species of plants, thus providing food for other species. **JUNGLE GYM** is the largest community-built playground in the United States. You can swing like a gibbon, run like the zebras and prowl around tiger-style in the 66,000-square foot playground. Jungle Gym features include: a 35-foot tall "Tree of Life" tree house structure; super slides, cargo netting and swings; a concrete sculpture garden, with a giant snake tunnel, bat cave, hippo and crocodile figures; dancing water fountain. **WILD ANIMAL CAROUSEL**. Visitors love taking rides on the 39 brightly-colored, wooden animals. The beautifully painted carousel features species found at the Zoo as well as several other exciting animals expected to arrive in the future. It is the first carousel in the country to offer the opportunity to ride a giant anteater or a clouded leopard cub.

OZ ARTS NASHVILLE
6172 Cockrill Bend Cir, Nashville, 615-350-7200
www.ozarts**nashville**.org
A new and unique destination for performing and visual art experiences. On-site eatery and bar.

ROLLER DERBY
Nashville Roller Girls
www.nashvillerollergirls.com

Nashville's only all-female, flat track roller derby league. They have 2 teams, with members separated by speed and skill level. Try to see the Music City All Stars—those girls are scary tough! Check out website for schedule and events listings.

RYMAN AUDITORIUM
116 Fifth Ave. N., Nashville, 615-889-3060
www.ryman.com
The "Mother Church of Country Music" was built in 1892 in what would become downtown Nashville by businessman Thomas G. Ryman as a venue for evangelist Sam Jones called the Union Gospel Tabernacle. (Don't you love that name?) From 1943-1974, it was the home of the Grand Ole Opry, the long-running, weekly radio showcase made up of a variety of big-name and smaller country acts.

A National Historic Landmark, the Ryman is open for tours. Costumes, programs and other memorabilia tied to performers such as Hank Williams, Minnie Pearl and Roy Acuff are prominently displayed on the first and second floors. The Ryman is also where Rayna (Britton) and Juliette (Panettiere) did the duet "Wrong Song" in the first season of the TV show "Nashville." Today, the Ryman only hosts the Grand Ole Opry between November and January. With the acoustics and the crescent arc to the pew seating, it's hard to find a bad seat. Depending on who's playing, tickets are sometimes available the day of the show. And you never know who will be playing.

TOMATO ART FEST
www.tomatoartfest.com

The Tomato Art Fest was founded by Meg and Bret MacFadyen, owners of East Nashville's <u>Art and Invention Gallery</u>. In 2004, the gallery hosted an art show celebrating the tomato in late summer, and planned a few neighborhood events to promote the show. The Tomato Art Fest proved so popular that it immediately turned into an annual, signature event for the hip, urban neighborhood of East Nashville. It's held in August.

WARNER PARK NATURE CENTER
7311 Highway 100, Nashville, 615-862-8555
<u>www.nashville.gov/</u>
This park is huge, and there's always something going on here. The Nature Center serves as a jumping-off point for exploring the 2,600 acres of Nashville's Percy Warner and Edwin Warner Parks. They have a wide range of environmental education programs, school field trips, educator training

workshops, outdoor recreation programs and other special activities for people of all ages. They also serve as a natural history and education reference center for individuals and groups. They promote and serve as a resource for organic gardening and native plant landscaping. Their campus includes the **Susanne Warner Bass Learning Center** which houses a natural history museum and programming space; the **Milbrey Warner Waller Library complete** with an extensive collection of natural history titles; the **Emily Warner Dean Administration Building**; a working organic garden including a greenhouse and a cedar shade house; a wildflower garden and fern garden; the Frist teaching pond; grounds landscaped with native plants; and the main trailhead for twelve miles of hiking trails.

YAZOO BREWING COMPANY
900 River Bluff Dr, Nashville, 615-891-4649
www.yazoobrew.com
NEIGHBORHOOD: Downtown; the Gulch
Though they went into business in 2003, as they expanded, they ended up moving into this building in 2010 so they could continue growing. Their taproom is open Wednesday through Friday evenings from 4-8pm, as well as Saturdays from 12-6 pm, serving their full lineup of beers. They also offer sampler trays so you can run the full gamut of their selections. You can order cheese plates, chips & salsa, spiced pecans, and beer bread - made with Yazoo of course. All food

items are locally made, locally grown. They offer a **WORKING BREWERY TOUR**, but check their web site for the schedule.

Chapter 6
SHOPPING & SERVICES

THE ARCADE

65, Arcade Alley, Nashville, 615-248-6673
www.nashvilledowntown.com/go/the-arcade
Located in the center of the downtown Nashville Arts
District, this historic shopping center hosts a variety
of arts events. Events include the Downtown
Nashville **First Saturday Art Crawl** (first Sat. of
every month from 6 – 9 p.m.). Eateries are on the first
floor, with some of the best galleries in town (about

15 of them) located upstairs. Food venues include the **Peach Cobbler Factory**, **Phillyman, Manny's House of Pizza**, the **Peanut Shop** and the Uptown Branch of the United States Postal Service.

ART & INVENTION GALLERY
1106 Woodland St, Nashville, 615-226-2070
www.artandinvention.com
NEIGHBORHOOD: East Nashville
Before the Five Points District of East Nashville became a hip, fun destination, they saw its potential. With that vision in mind, Bret and Meg MacFadyen converted an old garage at 1106 Woodland Street in 2000 into an artist's studio, which they named the *Garage Mahal*. Three years later, the *Art & Invention Gallery* was born. Having five to six shows annually, including the signature Tomato Art Show in August and Holiday Artisan Show in December, *Art & Invention Gallery* focuses on inventiveness in fine art, craft and original furniture. Adult and Children Workshops are held throughout the year as an outlet for creative energy.

BILLY REID
4015 Hillsboro Pike, Nashville, 615-292-2111
www.billyreid.com
NEIGHBORHOOD: Green Hills
Check out the Southern-inspired, hipster classics on sale here for men and women—shoes, heirloom, bags, jackets, blazers, shirts, caps, chinos, denim, accessories, gifts, Tees, outerwear.

GOODBUY GIRLS
1108 Woodland St, Nashville, 615-281-9447
www.goodbuygirlsnashville.com
Clothing shop for women that features a mix of
vintage and new clothing. It has about the best
selection of cowboy boots you'll find naywhere, some
with fringe, feathers, embroidery. (They are all used,
or as we say now, "pre-worn.")

GRIMEY'S
1060 E Trinity Ln, Nashville, 615-226-3811
www.grimeys.com
No question this is the best indie record store in
Nashville.

H. AUDREY
4027 Hillsboro Pike, Nashville, 615-760-5701
www.haudrey.com
NEIGHBORHOOD: Green Hills; Hill Center

The clothing scene has improved dramatically in recent years, a lot because of places like this one, which is run by Hank Williams's granddaughter, Holly. Rick Owens leather jackets, Haute Hippie, Rag & Bone and Helmut Lang—labels you expect to find in New York and L.A., but not here.

HIGH GARDEN
35 Woodland St, 615-919-4195
www.highgardentea.com
NEIGHBORHOOD: East End
A one-stop shopping destination for tea, but it's much more than that. Though you can't say tea is strictly good for medical reasons, here they have blends like "Clarity," which purports to help with skin problems. "Immortal Monk" is said to have an anti-aging effect. (Sign me up!) Here you can buy tea by the cup, the pot, by the bag, ounce, pound, and the selection is impressive. Large variety of loose leaf teas and herbs. Lovely atmosphere as well.

HILLSBORO VILLAGE
21st Ave, Nashville, No Phone
http://www.visitmusiccity.com/visitors/neighborhoods/hillsborovillage
NEIGHBORHOOD: 21st & Vanderbilt, Hillsboro, West End
A good shopping area that runs along 21st Avenue just below Vanderbilt. Lots of interesting little shops located here.

HIP ZIPPER VINTAGE

1008 Forrest Ave, Nashville, 615-228-1942
www.hipzipper.com
NEIGHBORHOOD: East Nashville
A place for high quality, reasonable priced vintage
clothing. Nashville's oldest all-vintage clothing shop.
They will buy men's & women's vintage clothing and
accessories from the 1930s to the 1980s. This
includes (but isn't limited to) ladies' dresses, lingerie,
swimsuits, sweaters, hats, purses, shoes, boots,
eyeglasses, belts, jewelry, as well as men's suits,
Western shirts, denim, cardigans, jackets, bow ties,
hats, eyeglasses belts and more.

IMOGENE & WILLIE
2601 12th Ave S, Nashville, 615-292-5005
www.imogeneandwillie.com
NEIGHBORHOOD: 12 South, Belmont, Hillsboro
In what used to be an old gas station is a hot shop where it's all about the jeans, blue and otherwise. Painstaking craftsmanship. Their tattooed staff will tailor your purchase specifically for you (but you might have to wait a few days to take it home—or have them ship it.) Denim for the most discriminating buyer (which means it's expensive). Clothes for men and women; lots of good gift ideas, too, if you look at their accessories. Some one-of-a-kind items, including hats, jackets, textiles, distressed leather trench boots. Definitely a must stop for the shopaholic.

LOCAL HONEY
2009 Belmont Blvd, Nashville, 615-690-6568
http://www.lhnashville.com/
NEIGHBORHOOD: Belmont, Hillsboro
This is a hair salon that doubles as a clothing store offering threads by local designers (as well as some vintage). I love this store.

MOTEL SHOPS
THE LOVELESS CAFÉ
8400 Hwy 100, Nashville, 615-646-9700
www.lovelesscafe.com
Before the Loveless Café got so famous, the 14 rooms
behind the place were rented out like any other motel.
Now they have been converted into a series of
privately owned shops that are a lot of fun to visit.
Hams & Jams Country Store is where you can get
not only the café's homemade preserves and country
hams, but also lot of gifts handmade by Tennessee
artisans, Loveless Café mugs and other merchandise
and souvenirs. Homemade pies and sweets. You can
get their pit-smoked BBQ here as well, by the pound
or in a sandwich. (I've come in here to get a sandwich
when the waiting line was too long at the café.)
Shimai Pottery & Gifts has great gift items. In
addition to their paintings, sculpture and tableware,
Shimai offers fine handcrafted jewelry, textiles,
shimmering hand-colored photographs and exquisite
carved wood. Features works from some of the area's
finest artisans. **Faithful Places** has timeless antiques,
books, home décor and accessories, gifts and unique
art objects.

NASHVILLE FARMERS' MARKET
900 Rosa Parks Blvd, Nashville, 615-880-2001
www.nashvillefarmersmarket.org
NEIGHBORHOOD: Downtown
The Farmers' Market in Nashville is really, really
beautiful. From the vendors in the covered space you
can buy your groceries, buy your vegetables and your
plants, preserves and jams, and then you can have
something to eat at one of the little indoor restaurants.
The fish places are fantastic, too.

OLD MADE GOOD
3701B Gallatin Pike, Nashville, 615-432-2882
www.oldmadegoodnashville.com/
A vintage goods boutique offering everything from
jewelry and clothing to handmade art and furniture,
some of it by local artisans. This is one of the hipper
stores in Nashville.

PEABODY SHOE REPAIR
718 Thompson Lane, Suite 105, Nashville, 615-292-5214
No Website
NEIGHBORHOOD: Hillsboro
There's a crusty old repairman in here who's worth the visit, but the reason I mention this place at all (since I don't expect you to take your shoes in here to get a shine) is that you can pick up a great pair of secondhand cowboy boots.

SAVANT VINTAGE
2302 12ᵗʰ Ave, Nashville, 615-385-0856
NEIGHBORHOOOD: 12 South, Belmont, Hillsboro

On the two floors of this big store you'll find a gargantuan selection of vintage items, from thousands of items of old clothing to shoes, furniture, accessories, you name it. Savant is known for being pricey (way pricey in some cases), but don't try to haggle with the owner. The prices are firm and she'll bite your neck off.

THIRD MAN RECORDS
623 7th Ave S, Nashville, 615-891-4393
www.thirdmanrecords.com
Open since 2009, this venue features a record store, record label offices, photo studio, dark room, and live venue. All records are recorded, printed and pressed in Nashville.

THOUSAND FACES
1720 21st Ave S, Nashville, 615) 298-3304
www.athousandfaces.com
NEIGHBORHOOD: Hillsboro/West End, 21st/Vanderbilt
A jumble of neat stuff for the gift giving connoisseur. Jewelry is a focal point with a selection not found on the beaten path. Pottery, glass, wood, metal, canvas and a great selection of cards are staples of this fun shop.

THE TURNIP TRUCK
The Turnip Truck Natural Market
701 Woodland St, Nashville, 615-650-3600
www.theturniptruck.com
NEIGHBORHOOD: Downtown, Gulch
More than just a wonderful health food market and store. One of the few places in town where you can get fresh juice made with organic produce. They use as much organic produce as we can. Occasionally, depending on the season, it is cost prohibitive for them to have 100% organic but they'll gladly let you

know on a day to day basis what is available. Here are some of their specialty blends: **The Doug Funny** has apples, lemon, carrots, beets, and ginger. **The Hulk** is made with cucumbers, kale, spinach, parsley, celery, apple, and lemon. **The Ninja Turtle** has celery, spinach, parsley, broccoli, and cucumber. **Mister Rogers** is a blend of carrots, apples, oranges, and celery.

UAL (United Apparel Liquidators)
2918 West End Ave, Nashville, 615-340-9999
www.shopual.com
Founded in 1980, this company now boasts 5 retail stores in 4 states. The store offers a great selection of high-end ladies' fashions at affordable prices. Think Chanel. Also carries overstocked item from nearby stores.

VENETIAN NAIL SPA
2114 Green Hills Village Drive, Nashville, 615-292-7727
www.venetiansalon.com
NEIGHBORHOOD: Green Hills
Nicole Kidman once got a manicure here when she was in town working on a movie. It's in the **Mall at Green Hills**, which has upscale stores like **Michael Kors** and **Louis Vuitton**, and is a great place for laid-back shopping and walking around.

INDEX

117

118

119

Other Books by
the Same Author

Andrew Delaplaine has written in widely varied fields: screenplays, novels
(adult and juvenile), travel writing, journalism. His books are available in
quality bookstores, libraries, as well as all online retailers.

JACK HOUSTON ST. CLAIR
POLITICAL THRILLERS

On Election night, as China and Russia mass soldiers on
their common border in preparation for war, there's a tie
in the Electoral College that forces the decision for
President into the House of Representatives as mandated

by the Constitution. The incumbent Republican President, working through his Aide for Congressional Liaison, uses the Keystone File, which contains dirt on every member of Congress, to blackmail members into supporting the Republican candidate. The action runs from Election Night in November to Inauguration Day on January 20. Jack Houston St. Clair runs a small detective agency in Miami. His father is Florida Governor Sam Houston St. Clair, the Republican candidate. While he tries to help his dad win the election, Jack also gets hired to follow up on some suspicious wire transfers involving drug smugglers, leading him to a sunken narco-sub off Key West that has $65 million in cash in its hull.

 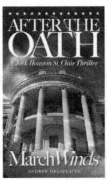 

AFTER THE OATH: DAY ONE
AFTER THE OATH: MARCH WINDS
WEDDING AT THE WHITE HOUSE

Only three months have passed since Sam Houston St. Clair was sworn in as the new President, but a lot has happened. Returning from Vienna where he met with Russian and Chinese diplomats, Sam is making his way back to Flagler Hall in Miami, his first trip home since being inaugurated. Son Jack is in the midst of turmoil of his own back in Miami, dealing with various dramas, not the least of which is his increasing alienation from Babylon Fuentes and his growing attraction to the seductive Lupe Rodriguez. Fernando Pozo addresses new problems as he struggles to expand Cuba's secret operations in the U.S., made even more difficult as U.S.-Cuban relations thaw. As his father returns home, Jack knows Sam will find as much trouble at home as he did in Vienna.

THE ADVENTURES OF SHERLOCK HOLMES THE 4TH

In this series, the original Sherlock Holmes's great-great-great grandson solves crimes and mysteries in the present day, working out of the boutique hotel he owns on South Beach.

THE BOSCOMBE VALLEY MYSTERY
Sherlock Holmes and Watson are called to a remote area of Florida overlooking Lake Okeechobee to investigate a murder

where all the evidence points to the victim's son as the killer. Holmes, however, is not so sure.

THE DEVIL'S FOOT

Holmes's doctor orders him to take a short holiday in Key West, and while there, Holmes is called on to look into a case in which three people involved in a Santería ritual died with no explanation.

THE CLEVER ONE

A former nun who, while still very devout, has renounced her vows so that she could "find a life, and possibly love, in the real world." She comes to Holmes in hopes that he can find out what happened to the man who promised to marry her, but mysteriously disappeared moments before their wedding.

THE COPPER BEECHES

A nanny reaches out to Sherlock Holmes seeking his advice on whether she should take a new position when her prospective employer has demanded that she cut her hair as part of the job.

THE RED-HAIRED MAN

A man with a shock of red hair calls on Sherlock Holmes to solve the mystery of the Red-haired League.

THE SIX NAPOLEONS

Inspector Lestrade calls on Holmes to help him figure out why a madman would go around Miami breaking into homes and businesses to destroy cheap busts of the French Emperor. It all seems very insignificant to Holmes—until, of course, a murder occurs.

THE MAN WITH THE TWISTED LIP

In what seems to be the case of a missing person, Sherlock Holmes navigates his way through a maze of perplexing clues that leads him through a sinister world to a surprising conclusion.

THE BORNHOLM DIAMOND

A mysterious Swedish nobleman requests a meeting to discuss a matter of such serious importance that it may threaten the line of succession in one of the oldest royal houses in Europe.

Made in the USA
Monee, IL
10 January 2020